The Art of Dying Well

Ideas and reflections
to help you face your death
with courage, peace and hope

Ian M Kilgour

Philip
Garside
Publishing Ltd.

Contact Ian at
127 Crossfield Road, Glendowie, Auckland 1071
phone: 027 271 7582
email: kilgours@xtra.co.nz

International print-on-demand paperback edition 2023
ISBN 9781991027559

Other editions

ISBN 9781988572048 Revised and expanded New Zealand paperback edition

ISBN 9781091701472 USA print-on-demand paperback

ISBN 9781988572055 PDF eBook

ISBN 9781988572062 ePub eBook

ISBN 9781988572079 Kindle eBook

Philip Garside Publishing Ltd
PO Box 17160
Wellington 6147
New Zealand

books@pgpl.co.nz — www.philipgarsidebooks.com

Contents

Preface

Everyone is on their own spiritual path and we all have different understandings of death, dying and life to come. Like-wise there are many different traditions, faiths and understandings around the mystery of death and beyond.

All the great faith traditions, such as Christianity, Hinduism, Islam, Judaism, Buddhism and Confucianism, have a wealth of understandings and material to help us navigate the final steps of our earthly journey. Embrace and be comfortable with your own understandings and convictions, but also be open to other insights and you'll be the richer for it.

The offerings of this book are intended as helpful pointers, not answers. May you enjoy the reflections and find peace and hope on your journey.

Keep a **notebook** or **journal** to hand, ready to write your thoughts and reflections as you read the book.

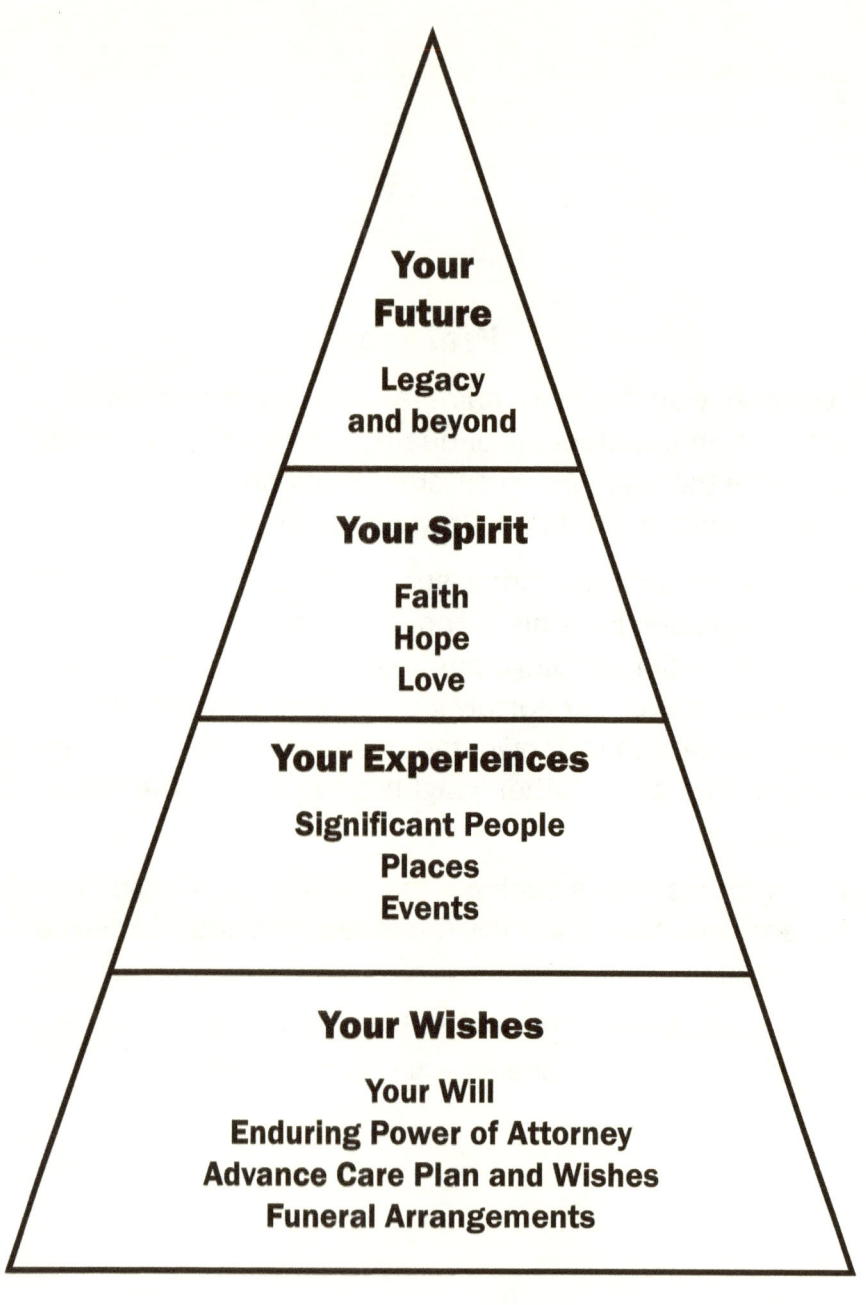

Your Future
Legacy
and beyond

Your Spirit
Faith
Hope
Love

Your Experiences
Significant People
Places
Events

Your Wishes
Your Will
Enduring Power of Attorney
Advance Care Plan and Wishes
Funeral Arrangements

Concept by Dr Stuart Crosbie

Introduction

Facing our death can generate questions, uncertainties, anxieties and fears. Some are about our loved ones and what will become of them, some are about how we will cope with the actual experience of dying and some are about what lies ahead of us when we die.

But facing our death can also be a wonderful time of personal reflection and deepening peace—when we gather together the many threads of our life, give voice to the love and gratitude that we have sometimes failed to express, and more and more let go into that 'ocean of love' from which we were born, to which we return and from which we can never be separated.

We all have to face our dying. As one wit once said, "Life is something none of us gets out of alive." This simple book is intended to help you face your own death with courage and faith, rather than with foreboding or fear. Some simple things can help ease your mind and bring peace to your heart.

Some of this book is written in the first-person singular to help you personalise your reflections. Feel free to dip into its pages just where and when you want, pondering only one or two paragraphs at a time.

A pyramid diagram has been included as a roadmap—building blocks, if you like—by which you can chart your progress through the various sections. I sincerely hope that these suggestions, explored and expanded with your own ideas, will be of real benefit to you.

The final part of this book includes readings and reflections from a wide range of perspectives and faith traditions.

Your Wishes

Your Will
Enduring Power of Attorney
Advance Care Plan and Wishes
Funeral Arrangements

Part 1 — Look forward, look back

Your wishes

It is important to make your wishes regarding your death and funeral known as clearly as possible. To that end, you may want to consider the following:

- Ensure your business and personal affairs are in order and that you have an updated Will.

- An Enduring Power of Attorney (EPA) is a legal document naming the person you'd like to take care of your personal and financial matters, if you can't. That person is called your Attorney and this can be set-up through your lawyer or filling out forms available online and lodging them with your lawyer.

- Fill out a document called 'Advance Care Plan' (available from your doctor). This allows you to state your preferences for palliative care if and when you are unable to express your own wishes.

- Distribute or record any personal items you'd like family or friends to have.

- Write or record a brief personal history. In years to come, your grandchildren and succeeding generations will thank you for this. Don't hesitate to ask someone to help you with this task.

- Write down any wishes you have regarding your funeral. This can include: readings, hymns, music, who you'd like to lead and participate in the service, where you want it held and in what form, and whether you want to be buried or cremated.

The Service or Event is about you and should reflect your interests and values and what you want. Planning a quiet family event or an exciting exit is a way to ensure you retain control of your life to the end.

An important consideration is to engage your loved ones in conversation about what's happening. Avoiding talk of the obvious is not helpful. Open conversation and planning reduce anxieties and assist grieving in a positive way.

- A 'good death' is where you can be comfortable, pain free, in a familiar place (if possible) and surrounded by those dearest to you. There need be no suffering. Palliative care will protect your dignity and will ensure death happens gently and peacefully which is the experience of the vast majority as they exit this life.

- It may also be helpful to those arranging your funeral to have a contact list (make this available before your death in writing or leave instructions as to where it can be found) of those whom you would like notified of your passing. You may also wish to choose, or have taken, some personal photos to have shown at your funeral service.

- Make sure that your family or whoever will be looking after your affairs, knows where to find important documents, computer passwords, etc. You may wish to make hard copies of these documents as a backup. Of course, be very careful with passwords, ensuring you keep these secure so that your privacy and access to your bank accounts, etc. remain secure.

- If you are on Facebook or other social media and wish not to have your page available after you've gone, be sure to delete it when the time is right or give someone else instructions and password access to do this on your behalf.

- Consider arranging a 'goodbye' event – a closure time with invited family and friends when all have an opportunity to express what is in their hearts to say. This can be a simple gathering of family and friends to celebrate your life by retelling the stories of your journey and reminiscing on times shared. It is helpful to have a trusted friend guide the event. Such an event is an honest way of facing what's happening and can be very helpful in adjusting everyone to the reality of the situation, and foster a positive grieving process.

- Last, but perhaps most important of all, find some one-on-one time with those nearest and dearest to you so that you can express your love and gratitude, and perhaps ask their forgiveness for any hurt you may have caused them. Be strong and supportive of your loved ones—they will be feeling their coming loss just as deeply as you are.

Record 'My Wishes' in your notebook

Your Experiences

Significant People
Places
Events

Your Wishes

Your Will
Enduring Power of Attorney
Advance Care Plan and Wishes
Funeral Arrangements

Your experiences

It can be very beneficial at this time to do a kind of 'life review'—taking a trip down memory lane and recalling the most memorable aspects of your life. As Carl Jung reminds us, "our vision will become clear only when we can look into our own heart. Who looks outside, dreams; who looks inside, awakes!"

Common to all people are three main categories of experience:

- Significant people
- Significant places
- Significant events.

During busier periods of life, we may have had little time to reflect on and evaluate such experiences in a more considered way. But now, as you rest, you have time and reason to look back and survey your personal life story.

You can trace the good times and bad, the highs and lows, joys and sorrows, excitements and disappointments, successes and failures, the pain and suffering, the losses and the grief– all that has served to shape you and make you the unique person you are today. Another word for 'unique' is 'precious.' And that's what you and your story are!

Your life story is unique and precious because there has never been, and never will be, anyone else with the same experience as yours. Your story will reflect a family history rich in its diversity, encompassing different countries and cultures, ethnicities and faith traditions, professions and occupations, migrants and pioneers, artists and musicians … and so much more.

To name, and perhaps write down, the significant people, places and events in your life is an important step in helping you bring your life to a close peacefully and with a sense of completion.

Memory exercises to gather up your experiences and achievements

The following are some exercises in 'remembering' to guide your reflections. There is no hurry. Just attempt one 'remembering' exercise at a time. It would be helpful to find a comfortable place and position. Close your eyes, try not to think too hard, and let the names, places and events float into your mind.

You'll notice through the next 'remembering' sections, the idea of having a notebook to write down the important wishes, people, places and events of your life. Having a special notebook or journal dedicated to this purpose can be of help and also be the place where you could record the memorable anecdotes of your life. It might even morph into the 'the story of my life!' This would be a lovely gift to leave your family and be appreciated by the generations to come. This doesn't have to be word perfect or typed. Doing it in your own hand writing even with corrections, would add to its appeal. I treasure the few samples of my parents' writing I still have.

Simply told stories of your life would give real insight into your own unique life and journey. When we think of it our lives are full of stories. These stories will also be from your parents and grandparents and the 'mega stories' of society that you've shared with countless other people. These guiding and shaping stories from your education and employment history, social, cultural, religious and community activities, have all helped to shape and give meaning and purpose to your life. Reflecting on them at this stage can be very rewarding particularly if you note down the stories that have mattered most to you and why.

My significant people

This 'remembering' is about the significant people in my life—those who have nurtured, guided, inspired and mentored me.

Parents, children and grandchildren, family members; neighbours, school teachers, Scouts, Guides, Boys and Girls Brigade leaders; Sunday school and Bible class teachers, sports coaches; friends and lovers, spouse/partner and soul mate; songwriters, musicians and singers; sporting heroes, movie and television stars, writers, artists, social reformers, politicians and world leaders. This list can even include people I didn't get on with, but from whom I learnt a great deal. Even faithful pets.

Another helpful exercise is to view or construct my family tree. In all probability one already exists that I can just add to. This will give context to the unfolding generations of which I am a vital and ongoing part.

Quietly and slowly I call these people to mind. I reflect on the contributions they've made to my life.

I name them and hold them in my mind and heart with a deep sense of gratitude and thankfulness for their part in my life's journey.

To more easily remember them, I will write down their names under a 'My significant people' heading in my notebook or journal.

Record 'My Significant People' in your notebook

My significant places

I will now remember the significant places in my history.

My birth place, where I began school, the houses and neighbourhoods where I lived, the roads where I walked or cycled to school, the sports clubs and fields where I played, the camps I attended, where I first learned to dance, where I first kissed a girl/boy, where I met my spouse/partner, our place of marriage, where I started work and subsequent places of employment and living, where we had our first child and other children.

Holiday places, mountains climbed, tours and countries visited. Places, places and more places!

Remembering my favourite music or contemplating my favourite place in the beauty of nature or my favourite art can take me places and help to bring me into a deep harmony with all things. Quietly, I will just let these significant places surface in my mind without too much thinking.

Some of those places may cause me to feel something of great value and reverence happened there. Where I sensed something of the 'divine presence' so these places are worth deeper reflection so as to discern what life was trying to say to me.

It will help if I write down these places under a 'My significant places' heading in my notebook or journal so I can easily return to them and ponder their deeper significance, calling to mind all the memories and feelings generated by these places.

> **Record 'My Significant Places'**
> **in your notebook**

My significant events

There are so many events in my life, but perhaps those that come most easily to mind do so because they mean something important to me. Many of my most memorable events connect with the significant people and places upon which I have already reflected.

My parents and the place of my birth. My first day at school, participating in my first school production, my first race, my first award at a prize giving. School balls, my friend's birthday parties. Obtaining my driver's license and taking the car out by myself for the first time. Passing an important exam. Graduation. My 21st birthday. My first successful job interview, my first job promotion. Leaving home, going flatting, overseas travel, my wedding day, our first home together, becoming a parent, christenings and baptisms, the death of parents, family members, friends and work colleagues, and many other red-letter events. Service Clubs, business associations and charities supported. Turning points in my life.

Quietly, I reflect on these significant events and try to re-enter these experiences to savour the moments that made them so memorable. Again, it will help to write these down. Looking at them may trigger other memories and their impact on me. In all these aspects of my past I see how incredibly connected all things are. I am part of a greater whole and will always be so. All of this gives me a profound sense of appreciation and gratitude for the life I have experienced.

Reflecting on these significant people, places and events is the stuff that has made up my life. Harvesting the challenges, learnings and blessings while being deeply thankful is the key to tapping into 'the wellspring of joy' – joy being a quality and experience of life that is beyond passing pleasure and happiness.

My part in the big picture of life

Having reflected on the people, places and events of my life I can now see myself in the big picture of life.

I want to value this world I live in as the one I know and treasure. It is the physical foundation of my life. Being grounded in this reality helps me see myself as part of the greater whole. I am made of 'star dust,' the very essence of the universe. However small I feel myself to be, I am an important part of this whole.

My cells, molecules and organs are all part of this living, breathing continuum of life and will always be so. My body will die and return to the dust of the universe and go on to be a part of the continuing and remarkable story of the cosmos. My spirit – what makes me, me – will also continue as it is re-absorbed into the memory, energy and consciousness of the universe.

Put in a more traditional way, I return to the Creator who gave me life. With a sense of awe and wonder and with deep thankfulness I see myself as being a conscious part of all that is and realise I will continue to be so, although in what form I don't know. I sense the union I have with this vast ocean of becoming and feel the anticipation of greater things to come. As Margaret Fuller observed, "there is nothing in a caterpillar that tells you it's going to be a butterfly!"

Some people are troubled by the use of the word 'God,' often because it conjures up negative notions of reward or punishment from some authoritarian Super-Being, perhaps instilled in us by over demanding parents or religious zealots. It is helpful to realise that there are many valid names and ways to express the varieties of our human and religious experience. The Jews considered the name God too sacred to utter or write and so used substitutes such as Jehovah and Yahweh. Muslims have 99 names for Allah.

Descriptions like; the Beyond within, the Ground of our being, the Divine Presence, Universal Love, Transcendent Other, Creator Spirit, Providence, the ever present Mystery of Promise, can be helpful alternatives to expand our thinking or that better represent our understandings.

A human being is part of the whole,
called by us 'Universe,'
a part limited in time and space.
He experiences himself, his thoughts and feelings
as something separated from the rest—
a kind of optical delusion of his consciousness.
This delusion is a kind of prison for us,
restricting us to our personal desires
and to affection for a few persons nearest to us.
Our task must be to free ourselves from this prison.

Albert Einstein (1879–1955)

There is an endless net of threads
throughout the universe.
The horizontal threads are in space.
The vertical threads are in time.
At every crossing of the threads, there is an individual,
and every individual is a crystal bead.
And every crystal bead reflects not only the light from
every other crystal in the net,
but also every other reflection throughout
the entire universe.

Rig Veda

The progress of our soul is like a perfect poem.
It has an infinite idea which once realised makes all
movements full of meaning and joy.

Rabindranath Tagore (1861 – 1941)

I think over again my small adventures, my fears,
those small ones that seemed so big,
all those vital things I had to get and to reach,
and yet there is only one great thing:
to live and see the great day that dawns,
and the light that fills the world.

Old Inuit Song

Surfacing the hard stuff and valuing myself

I need to be aware that the process of remembering can surface feelings of guilt and regret about past failures, broken relationships, hurts and disappointments. These, too, are part of who I am, and I need to own them.

I need to embrace my past, hurts, failures, disappointments and all. But I do not need to give them oxygen by rehearsing them negatively over and over again. Reflecting on what I have learned from these episodes, I can let them go. I can imagine opening a window and casting them out never to be entertained again.

Experience over the years reveals that across the shoreline of everyone's life lie broken and sharp pieces of human experience that people discard or bury in the hope of forgetting. Left in this state those pieces can remain troublesome and dangerous.

But there is another way to treat these pieces. When I am accepting of life as it is, and trust myself to life, I come to find all those pieces can be re-shaped into a new plan and purpose of beauty and great worth. I then can enter into the relieving experience of forgiving others and knowing myself forgiven.

Elisabeth Kübler-Ross spoke about people being like stained glass windows. They sparkle and shine when the sun is out, but when the darkness sets in, their true beauty is revealed only if there is a light within.

I can allow who I am to be accepted, valued and loved. I don't have to do anything to prove my worth. I am worthy of love, acceptable, beautiful, whole and part of divine life. This need to trust and accept my own self-worth can be greatly assisted when I can acknowledge the beauty and worth in others, acknowledging they too have had a unique journey that has made them who they are.

When bodies and brains wear out

Another aspect of the 'hard stuff' is when I face my departure from this world because of chronic illness or the aging process. The breaking down of my body and mind brings with it all sorts of challenges, difficulties and discomfort, not to mention aches and pains and forgetfulness. With strokes, heart attacks and arthritis I fear losing my independence. It is said, "getting old is not for the faint hearted" and that is very true. But as many things in life are inevitable and I have little control over such matters, I have to develop ways of coping and this can evoke undiscovered strength of character and determination. By coming to accept and even embrace the sorrows of life I can gain an enduring sense of peace.

There are two things I can do that can be helpful.

Firstly, reflect on the rhythms of life. When young I was totally dependent on the care of my parents and when I had children, they were totally dependent on me. Life repeats itself and I come to be dependent again on those I love and who care for me. They step up up to do the task of caring which I need to accept with good grace. Life has a built-in reciprocity.

Secondly, though my body and mind is in a state of deterioration, my essential spirit, what makes me who I am, remains completely whole. I can think of a shattered glass window representing my failing mind. People on either side looking at and talking to me only see a fragmented image of me but in reality, I am still whole. So, I will journey within myself to my inner being and take comfort in the spiritual reality of your wholeness.

'Mid all the traffic of the ways,
Turmoils without, within,
Make in my heart a quiet place,
And come and dwell therein.

A little shrine of quietness,
All sacred to Thyself,
Where Thou shalt all my soul possess,
And I may find myself.

A little shelter from life's stress,
Where I may lay me prone,
And bare my soul in loneliness,
And know as I am known.

A little place of mystic grace,
Of self and sin swept bare,
Where I may look upon Thy face,
And talk with Thee in prayer.

Come, occupy my silent place,
And make thy dwelling there!
More grace is wrought in quietness
Than any is aware.

John Oxenham (1852–1941)

Record 'My Thoughts' in your notebook

Loving with human love,
one may pass from love to hatred;
but divine love cannot change.
Nothing, not even death, can shatter it.
It is the very nature of the soul ... Love is life.
All, all that I understand,
I understand only because I love.
All is bound up in love alone.
Love is God, and dying means for me a particle of love,
to go back to the universal and eternal source of love.

Leo Tolstoy (1828–1910)

I hold it true, whate'er befall;
I feel it, when I sorrow most;
'Tis better to have loved and lost
Than never to have loved at all.

Alfred, Lord Tennyson (1809–1892)

Thou, our Elder Brother, Who
In Thy flesh our trial knew,
Thou who hast been touched by these
Our most sad infirmities,
Thou alone the grief can span
In the dual heart of man,
And between the soul and sense
Reconcile all difference,　,
Change the dream of me and mine
For the truth of Thee and Thine,
And through chaos, doubt and strife
Interfuse Thy calm of life.

John Greenleaf Whittaker (1807–1892)

Because I have loved life, I shall have no sorrow to die.
I have sent up my gladness on wings,
to be lost in the blue of the sky.
I have run and leaped with the rain,
I have taken the wind to my breast.
My cheek like a drowsy child to the face of the earth
I have pressed.
Because I have loved life, I shall have no sorrow to die.

I have kissed young love on the lips,
I have heard his song to the end.
I have struck my hand like a seal
in the loyal hand of a friend.
I have known the peace of heaven,
the comfort of work done well.
I have longed for death in the darkness
and risen alive out of hell.
Because I have loved life, I shall have no sorrow to die.

I give a share of my soul to the world
where my course is run.
I know that another shall finish the task
I must leave undone.
I know that no flower, nor flint was in vain
on the path I trod.
As one looks on a face through a window,
through life I have looked on God.
Because I have loved life, I shall have no sorrow to die.

Amelia Josephine Burr (1878–1968)

Facing the big questions

The inevitability of our dying may bring to mind the big philosophical and religious imponderables – questions such as: Who am I? Where did I come from? What is the purpose and meaning of life, if indeed there is any? Is there God and, if so, what is God's nature?

Not finding at least partial answers to these questions can produce a sense of futility and hopelessness about life. If, after all our living and loving, our best efforts to work, provide and survive, if it all just comes to naught, what then?

Even if we choose to believe that there is no grander scheme beyond what we've known here, that need not diminish the significance of our journey on this planet. We can value it because it's the only life we will ever have. To reflect on what we've enjoyed and achieved is to be content and fulfilled.

> Dust as we are, the immortal spirit grows
> Like harmony in music; there is a dark
> Inscrutable workmanship that reconciles
> discordant elements, makes them cling together
> in one society. How strange that all
> the terrors, pains and early miseries,
> regrets, vexations, lassitudes interfused
> within my mind, should e'er have borne a part;
> And that a needful part, in making up
> The calm existence that is mine when I
> Am worthy of myself! Praise to the end!
>
> *William Wordsworth (1770–1850)*

Record 'My Thoughts' in your notebook

Leaving this world

I came into this world with nothing and when I depart this world, I'll take nothing with me. While this is true of my body and material possessions, it is not true of my spirit and character, or of my memories and what has made me who I am—a unique, loved and precious person.

I will take with me what I've made of myself and what life has shaped me to be. As I've seen from my 'remembering' exercises, my life has been a rich and remarkable tapestry woven of all those significant people, places and events of my life and all that I've done and achieved. Whatever my experience, views, church tradition, religion or none, I can take heart from all that has sustained me and given me strength and encouragement throughout my life.

I trust that the life to which I go will be a place or state where the broken things are mended and the lost things found, where all I have hoped and willed of good shall exist, where the dream will come true and the ideal be realised, where I will be at home with those dearest to me and to dwell in the completeness of love.

If at my birth I had known what would unfold, I would not have believed it. Now, departing this life I can go in confidence and with hope, knowing this is not the end of life but the start of an endless adventure. As Eckhart Tolle argues:

> Death is not the opposite of life.
> Life has no opposite.
> The opposite of death is birth.
> Life is eternal.

I have seen death too often to believe in death.
It is not an ending—but a withdrawal.
As one who finishes a long journey,
Stills the motor,
Turns off the lights,
Steps from the car,
And walks up the path
To the home that awaits.

Author unknown

Within us is the soul of the whole, the wise silence,
the universal beauty, the eternal One.

Ralph Waldo Emerson (1803–1882)

Death is not the light going out.
It is the lamp being switched off
because the dawn has come.

Rabindranath Tagore (1861–1941)

When it comes your time to die,
be not like those whose hearts are filled
with the fear of death,
so that when their time comes,
they weep and pray for a little more time
to live their lives over again in a different way.
Sing your death song and die like a hero going home.

Chief Tecumseh, Shawnee Nation (1768-1813)

Record 'My Thoughts' in your notebook

The Lord who created you says,
"Do not be afraid – I will save you.
I have called you by name – you are mine.
When you pass through deep waters, I will be with you;
your troubles will not overwhelm you.
When you pass through fire, you will not be burned;
the hard trials that come will not hurt you.
For I am the Lord your God, who saves you
and sets you free;
I will save your life, because you are precious to me
and because I love you and give you honour.
Do not be afraid - I am with you!"

Isaiah 43:1-5 Good News Translation

O God let me rise to the edges of time
and open my life to your eternity.
Let me run to the edges of space
and gaze at your immensity;
Let me climb through the barriers of sound
and pass into your silence,
And then, in stillness and silence let me adore you,
Who are Life – Light – Love – without beginning
and without end,
The Source – the Sustainer – the Restorer –
the Purifier – of all that is.
The Love who has bound earth to heaven
by the beams of a cross;
The Healer who has renewed a dying race
by the blood of a chalice;
The God who has taken humankind into glory
by the wounds of sacrifice,
God ... God .... God ...Blessed be God.
Let me adore you. Amen

Sister Ruth SLG

Your Spirit

Faith
Hope
Love

Your Experiences

Significant People
Places
Events

Your Wishes

Your Will
Enduring Power of Attorney
Advance Care Plan and Wishes
Funeral Arrangements

Part 2 — Your spirit

Many people believe that our story doesn't end with death—that there is life beyond this life. This section deals with 'spiritual understandings' about death and dying, and the prospect of another life to come.

Reasons for hope

Throughout the long history of humankind there has been a deeply held belief in something beyond our mortal existence. There is a conviction and intuition deep in the human heart that the process of dying leads to something else and that this will be as astounding as our birth.

Before birth we had no idea what lay ahead of us outside of the womb. So, too, our dying may – to our surprise – birth us into some new form of life.

Sacred writings from many faith traditions do their best to 'express the inexpressible' in human imagery and language. Your culture or religion will have its own symbols and ways of celebrating life and preparing for death. I invite you to reflect on what they mean to you – your cultural and faith tradition will be rich in meanings.

At best, though, these are human concepts and language, struggling to express and give form to the mystery of life and death. Religious thought and sacred writings have given many answers to the big questions, but for the most part they are human constructions and conclusions. Thankfully, divine inspiration and light sometimes breaks through the words and images and provides a sense of hope and vision that there is much more to come.

All shall be well, and all shall be well,
and all manner of things shall be well ...
for there is a Force of Love moving through the
universe that holds us fast and will never let us go.

Julian of Norwich, (1342–1416)

Our future – a spiritual perspective

Jesus was known as a wandering wisdom teacher, healer
and spiritual person who spoke about 'the Kingdom of God'
and 'eternal life.' His teachings indicate that he understood
'eternal life' to be more about the 'quality of life now,' rather
than just some everlasting life to come. For example the
prayer he taught his disciples to pray says, "Your kingdom
come; your will be done **on earth** as it is in heaven."

Jesus, Buddha, Confucius, Muhammed, to name just a
few – gifted us understandings that have enhanced our
experience of this world yet can also be described as
'the quality of life that transcends death.' Unfortunately,
religious followers have sometimes developed distorted
views of these sublime teachings and subscribed instead to
beliefs that generate fear and guilt and make it difficult for
some people to die in peace.

I have felt a presence that disturbs me with the joy
Of elevated thoughts, a sense sublime
Of something far more deeply interfused,
Whose dwelling is the light of setting suns
And the round ocean, and the living air,
And the blue sky, and in the mind of man,
A motion and a spirit that impels
All thinking things, all objects of all thought,
And rolls through all things.

William Wordsworth (1770–1850)

Beyond the farthest bounds of earth,
Beyond the ocean's line,
Beyond the starlit universe
We sense a power divine.

The lines and circles, planes and arcs
Which we by science trace
All indicate a master mind,
Its beauty, truth and grace.

Like searching eyes earth's telescopes
The fiery heavens scan;
And now the music of the spheres
Is heard by listening man.

Lord, as we seek for vaster truth,
And as our spaceships soar,
Help us to recognize your might
And praise your mercy more.

For you, who set the ordinance
Of worlds beyond our sight,
Have given us minds desiring truth
And hearts that know delight.

Lord, teach us in your only Son
To reach the way we dream,
To follow truth as he knew truth,
And find the life supreme.

Miriam M. Richards (1918–1989)

Doorways into the mystery of God

We know so little about 'life beyond' and it is unwise to do much speculating. It seems clear that Jesus believed in a life to come, but he gave few details. Perhaps Jesus realised that if we knew too much about what lay on the other side, it would reduce our willingness to cope with the hard stuff of this life and lead us to give up our hold on life too easily. Jesus suggested instead that we should have faith in him as showing us "the way, the truth and the life."

The love experienced in Jesus and taught by all great spiritual leaders, excludes no one. Love and grace are both personal and universal, arising from the nature of the God in whom they believed. Christ's emphasis was more on having a loving relationship with God and each other, than with having a correct belief system.

Spiritual wellbeing
is the affirmation of life
in a relationship to
God, self, community and the environment
that nurtures and celebrates wholeness.
It is the strong sense that I am 'held'
by someone greater than myself
who nurtures the whole creation,
giving life meaning and purpose.
It is the sure knowledge that I am
part of that meaning and purpose.

Author Unknown

A deeply personal experience

Do you remember the lyrics of the popular song:

> Put your hand in the hand of the man who stilled
> the water, put your hand in the hand of the man who
> stilled the sea.

This same intimacy comes into focus in the well-known words of the 23rd Psalm:

> Though I walk through the valley
> of the shadow of death,
> I will fear no evil because you are with me,
> your rod and staff comfort me.

How personal is this!

• • •

> Give us, ever patient God,
> that spirit which can endure delay,
> and bear suffering and never give in.
> To endure delay, and live through each moment
> with confidence,
> and not lose heart, nor allow the vision
> of better times to fade.
> To bear suffering, yet not be broken by it,
> and not be overcome by bitterness,
> nor find faith fall short.
> And never give in, yet not to bear a grudge
> and not to live,
> grim faced, stiff-lipped, nor show pride in enduring,
> But rather, by your Spirit, point to Jesus our Lord who,
> through temptations, injustice,
> hardship and opposition
> patiently bore your perfect will and with constant
> hope.

Author Unknown

I said to the man who stood at the gate of the year,
'Give me a light that I may tread safely
into the unknown.'

And he replied: 'Go out into the darkness
and put your hand in the hand of God.

That shall be to you better than a light
and safer than a known way!'

Minnie Louise Haskins (1875–1957)

And Him evermore we
behold walking in Galilee,
Through the waving cornfield's gold,
By hamlet and wood and wold,
By the side of the marvellous sea.
He touches the sightless eyes
Before Him the demons flee.
To the dead He sayeth, "Arise,"
To the living, "Follow Me."
And His voice still soundeth on
From centuries that have gone
To the centuries that shall be.

Henry Wadsworth Longfellow (1807–1882)

The intimacy of prayer

Prayer is the primary way in which people can have a conversation with their God. We could just as easily use meditation. Prayer need not be in words; it can be in the quietness of the heart seeking a sense of 'Presence' and being at one with God or Life – whichever term you feel more comfortable with. Howard Thurman put it well when he said:

> In the stillness of the quiet, if we listen,
> we can hear the whisper of the heart
> giving strength to weakness,
> courage to fear, hope to despair.

Prayers are not about getting what we want but to help us know our inner being. Meister Eckhart, a mystic from the middle ages said:

> If the only prayer you ever say in your entire life is thank you, it will be enough. It may help to understand prayer as 'thinking in the presence of God.'

Music, too, can often bring us into a deep sense of harmony and oneness with all things. As Plato said:

> Music is a moral law. It gives a soul to the universe, wings to the mind, flight to the imagination, a charm to sadness, and life to everything.

• • •

The highest form of prayer is not a prayer for anything.
It is a deep and profound silence,
in which we allow ourselves to be still
and know our God.
In that silence we are changed, we are calmed,
we are illumined.
In the castle of my heart there is a little postern gate
Where, when I enter, I am in the presence of God.
In a moment, in the turning of a thought,
I am where God is.
When I meet God there, all life gains a new meaning,
Small things become great, and great things small.
Lowly and despised things are shot through with glory.
My troubles seem like pebbles on the road,
My joys seem like everlasting hills,
All my fever is gone in the great peace of God,
And I pass through the door from time to Eternity.

Walter Rauschenbusch (1861–1918)

Teach us, O God, that silent language
which says all things.
Teach our souls to remain silent in your presence;
That we might adore you in the deeps of our being
and await all things from you while asking nothing
but the accomplishment of your will.
Teach us to remain quiet
under your action and produce
in our souls that deep and simple prayer
which specifies nothing and expresses everything.

Jean Nicholas Grou (1731–1803)

Faith and trust

It is helpful to think of faith as the way of the heart. It is not about believing certain creeds or doctrines of a church or religion. 'To believe,' as that word was used in the New Testament, originally meant 'to belove.' What we believe, in other words, is what we love most. Faith is about 'loving your God' and the qualities and values of God's Kingdom— or as some say, 'God's **Kin**-dom,' which speaks more of family and relationships.

Remember faith and hope is not believing everything will turn out well but more the conviction that what you believe makes sense regardless of how it turns out. Be strong in what you believe and belove!

An Affirmation of Faith

We believe in a God who always surprises us,
who creates life from death,
who brings good out of evil.
Who leads us from despair to hope.
We believe in a God who is faithful to us,
who shows us mercy when we run away,
who shows us patience when we deny the truth,
who gives reconciling love when we betray.
We believe in a God who lived and died as one of us
to take the fear out of living and dying,
to open our eyes to death,
within us and around us,
and open our hearts to new ways of living.
We believe in a God who forgives us,
who sets us free from past grief and failure
and calls us forth into a new day.

Source unknown

Your
Future

Legacy
and beyond

Your Spirit

Faith
Hope
Love

Your Experiences

Significant People
Places
Events

Your Wishes

Your Will
Enduring Power of Attorney
Advance Care Plan and Wishes
Funeral Arrangements

A love with no limits

Love knows no limit to its endurance,
no end to its trust, no fading of its hope;
it can outlast anything.
It is, in fact, the one thing that still stands
when all else has fallen...
Meanwhile these three remain:
faith, hope, and love;
and the greatest of these is love.

1 Corinthians 13: 7-8a, 13
J.B.Phillips New Testament / Good News Translation

If love should count you worth and should deign
One day to seek your door and be your guest,
Pause! Ere you draw the bolt and bid him rest,
If in your old content you would remain,
For not alone He enters; in his train
Are angels of the mist, the lonely quest
Dreams of the unfulfilled and unpossessed,
And sorrow, and life's immemorial pain.
He wakes desires you never may forget,
He shows you stars you never saw before.
He makes you share with Him, for evermore,
The burden of the world's regret.
How wise you were to open not! and yet,
How poor if you should turn Him from the door!

Sidney Royse Lysaght (1860–1941)

Just think how love has sustained you throughout your life. How hope has been present as you've worked to provide for your family, building a future and hoping for the best of outcomes. How, by your faithfulness to duty as a spouse, parent, grandparent, brother, sister, friend, work colleague, you have supported those in relationship with you. And not just faithfulness, but how having faith in principles, values, people and God has kept you going through good times and bad in your pursuit of goodness, truth and beauty. If you find the word 'God' unhelpful, think rather of love and the highest values and principles that have given your life meaning and purpose or understand the word 'God' not as a noun but as a verb that invites us to live and love to the fullest.

All this love that you have shared with others will always be—all the memories will continue on. You will live on in the hearts of everyone you have touched and nurtured. Death ends our life here, but our love continues on through generations to come. As Thomas Campbell said, "To live in hearts we leave behind, is not to die." We continue to live in the memory of life, both in time and eternity.

> But as it is written, eye hath not seen, nor ear heard,
> neither has it entered into the heart of man,
> the things which God has prepared for them
> that love him.
>
> *1 Corinthians 2: 9 (King James Version)*

A love stronger than death

> I consider that what we suffer at this present time
> cannot be compared at all with the glory
> that is going to be revealed to us ...
> In view of all this, what can we say?
> If God is for us, who can be against us?...
> Who, then, can separate us from the love of Christ?
> Can trouble do it, or hardship or persecution
> or hunger or poverty or danger or death?...
> No, in all these things we have complete victory
> through him who loved us!
> For I am certain that nothing can separate us
> from his love:
> neither death nor life, neither angels
> nor other heavenly rulers or powers,
> neither the present nor the future,
> neither the world above nor the world below –
> there is nothing in all creation
> that will ever be able to separate us
> from the love of God
> which is ours through Christ Jesus our Lord.

Romans 8: 18, 31, 35, 37–39 (Good News Translation)

I believe that whether you are Christian or not, you cannot be separated from the Love of God and will be accompanied by the presence of the One who was called 'Immanuel', which means 'God with us,' and who said, "I am with you always, to the end of the age." This sense of the 'divine presence' has been experienced by people of faith and no faith because we are talking about the fundamental source of life, love and energy in all things.

As St. John says,

So we have known and believe the love that God has for us. God is love, and those who abide in love abide in God, and God abides in them.

1 John 4: 16

• • •

Life is a journey on many different roads
but God is always with us
Sometimes we lift our faces to the sun
and God is with us
But then there is the hard journey
through the pathways of pain
and fears in dark places.
But God is with us.
Nothing can separate us
from the love of God in Christ Jesus.

Pitt Street Uniting Church Liturgy

By night or by day, or by circumstance;
Neither in the silence, Nor in the city's roar;
Nor as I lie at the door of death,
Or stand on the threshold of a new life;
For You are with me, around me,
underneath me, bearing me up,
Giving me strength, luring me on.
I am not alone;
You have been, You will be, You are with me.
'Lo, I am with you always, even unto the
end of the world.'

Author Unknown

Record 'My Thoughts' in your notebook

Part 3 — Reflect and contemplate

It would be helpful to realise that some of the theology and language of the readings, poetry and hymns featured in this section are from a different time and context in history and may conflict with our understandings today. Yet there remains great blessing and richness to be found in these words, which have sustained many through the ages. All Biblical passages are from the NRSV translation.

Scripture Readings from Faith Traditions

Readings from the Jewish Scriptures

The Lord is my shepherd, I shall not want.
He makes me lie down in green pastures;
he leads me beside still waters;
he restores my soul.
He leads me in right paths
for his name's sake.
Even though I walk through the darkest valley,
I fear no evil;
for you are with me;
your rod and your staff – they comfort me.
You prepare a table before me
in the presence of my enemies;
you anoint my head with oil;
my cup overflows.
Surely goodness and mercy shall follow me
all the days of my life,
and I shall dwell in the house of the Lord
my whole life long.

Psalm 23

The Lord is merciful and gracious,
slow to anger and abounding in steadfast love.
He does not deal with us according to our sins,
nor repay us according to our iniquities.
For as the heavens are high above the earth,
so great is his steadfast love toward
those who fear him;
as far as the east is from the west,
so far he removes our transgressions from us.

As a father has compassion for his children,
so the Lord has compassion for those who fear him.
For he knows how we were made;
he remembers that we are dust.

As for mortals, their days are like grass;
they flourish like a flower of the field;
for the wind passes over it, and it is gone,
and its place knows it no more.

But the steadfast love of the Lord is from
everlasting to everlasting
on those who fear him,
and his righteousness to his children's children,
to those who keep his covenant
and remember to do his commandments.

Psalm 103

I lift up my eyes to the hills—
from where will my help come?
My help comes from the Lord,
who made heaven and earth.

He will not let your foot be moved;
he who keeps you will not slumber.
He who keeps Israel
will neither slumber nor sleep.

The Lord is your keeper;
the Lord is your shade at your right hand.
The sun shall not strike you by day,
nor the moon by night.

The Lord will keep you from all evil;
he will keep your life.
The Lord will keep your going out and your coming in
from this time on and forever more.

Psalm 121

O Lord, you have searched me and known me.
You know when I sit down and when I rise up;
you discern my thoughts from far away.
You search out my path and my lying down,
and are acquainted with all my ways.
Even before a word is on my tongue,
O Lord, you know it completely.
You hem me in, behind and before,
and lay your hand upon me.
Such knowledge is too wonderful for me;
it is so high that I cannot attain it...

For it was you who formed my inward parts;
you knit me together in my mother's womb.
I praise you, for I am fearfully and wonderfully made.
Wonderful are your works;
that I know very well.
My frame was not hidden from you,
when I was being made in secret,
intricately woven in the depths of the earth.
Your eyes beheld my unformed substance.
In your book were written
all the days that were formed for me,
when none of them as yet existed.
How weighty to me are your thoughts, O God!
How vast is the sum of them!
I try to count them—they are more than the sand;
I come to the end—I am still with you.

Search me, O God, and know my heart;
test me and know my thoughts.
See if there is any wicked way in me,
and lead me in the way everlasting.

Psalm 139: 1–6, 13–18, 23–24

There is a time for everything
There is a time for moving and making new start.

There is a time for packing up and saying goodbye.
There are times for strong debate and disagreement.

There are times for mending rifts and healing.
There is a time for sorrow and weeping,
There is a time for laughing and joy.
There is a time for the bliss of young love.
There is a time for cuddling small children.
There is a time for finding new understandings.

Losing things and forgetting are part of life's rhythm.
There is a time for conserving all we have.
There comes a time for sorting out and throwing away.
There is a time for tearing up old clothes and old ideas.
There is a time for reclaiming virtues long forgotten.

Keeping our thoughts to ourselves has its place in life.
On other occasions we must speak plainly.
Sadly, there is a time for war.
Gladly, there is a time for peace.

It seems there is a right time for everything.
We desire to know the future, but this knowledge is
beyond us.
So we must do the best with what we have as day
follows day.
If today is one of your better days, enjoy life's riches.
If today is dark with sadness or regret, quite simply,
your work is to hold on until you find the light again.
Don't waste your tears; your troubles can be a tutor.
Through tears new insights come.
Remember this...God is love.
Love is at the heart of the universe and only what is
done in love endures.

Ecclesiastes 3. Adapted by Reverend Stan Stewart

Readings from the Christian New Testament

Do not let your hearts be troubled.
Believe in God, believe also in me.
In my Father's house there are many dwelling places.
If it were not so, would I have told you
that I go to prepare a place for you?
And if I go and prepare a place for you,
I will come again and will take you to myself,
so that where I am, there you may be also.
And you know the way to the place where I am going.
Thomas said to him,
"Lord, we do not know where you are going.
How can we know the way?"
Jesus said to him, "I am the way, and the truth, and
the life."

John 14: 1–6

Jesus said... "Come to me, all you that are weary
and are carrying heavy burdens,
and I will give you rest.
Take my yoke upon you, and learn from me;
for I am gentle and humble in heart,
and you will find rest for your souls.
For my yoke is easy, and my burden is light."

Matthew 11: 28-30

When Jesus saw the crowds, he went up the mountain;
and after he sat down, his disciples came to him.
Then he began to speak, and taught them, saying:

"Blessed are the poor in spirit,
for theirs is the kingdom of heaven.

Blessed are those who mourn,
for they will be comforted.

Blessed are the meek [humble],
for they will inherit the earth.

Blessed are those who hunger and thirst for righteousness, for they will be filled.

Blessed are the merciful,
for they will receive mercy.

Blessed are the pure in heart,
for they will see God.

Blessed are the peacemakers,
for they will be called children of God.

Blessed are those who are persecuted for righteousness' sake,
for theirs is the kingdom of heaven.

Blessed are you when people revile you and persecute you and utter all kinds of evil against you falsely on my account.

Rejoice and be glad, for your reward is great in heaven,
for in the same way they persecuted the prophets who were before you."

Matthew 5: 1–12
The Beatitudes

What then are we to say about these things?
If God is for us, who is against us?

Who will separate us from the love of Christ?
Will hardship, or distress, or persecution,
or famine, or nakedness, or peril, or sword?

No, in all these things we are more than conquerors
through him who loved us.
For I am convinced that neither death, nor life,
nor angels, nor rulers, nor things present,
nor things to come,
nor powers, nor height, nor depth,
nor anything else in all creation,
will be able to separate us from the love of God
in Christ Jesus our Lord.

Romans 8: 31, 35, 37–39

Then I saw a new heaven and a new earth;
for the first heaven and the first earth
had passed away,
and the sea was no more.
And I saw the holy city, the new Jerusalem,
coming down out of heaven from God,
prepared as a bride
adorned for her husband.
And I heard a loud voice from the throne saying,

"See, the home of God is among mortals.
He will dwell with them;
they will be his peoples,
and God himself will be with them;
he will wipe every tear from their eyes.
Death will be no more;
mourning and crying and pain will be no more,
for the first things have passed away."

Revelation 21: 1–4

Love is patient; love is kind;
love is not envious
or boastful or arrogant or rude.
It does not insist on its own way;
it is not irritable or resentful;
it does not rejoice in wrong doing
but rejoices in the truth.
It bears all things, believes all things,
hopes all things, endures all things.
Love never ends.
But as for prophecies, they will come to an end;
as for tongues, they will cease;
as for knowledge, it will come to an end.

For we know only in part,
and we prophesy only in part;
but when the complete comes,
the partial will come to an end.
When I was a child, I spoke like a child,
I thought like a child, I reasoned like a child;
when I became an adult,
I put an end to childish ways.
For now we see in a mirror, dimly,
but then we will see face to face.
Now I know only in part;
then I will know fully, even as I have been fully known.

And now faith, hope, and love abide, these three;
and the greatest of these is love.

1 Corinthians 13: 4–13

Rejoice in the Lord always; again, rejoice.
Let your gentleness be known to everyone.
The Lord is near. Do not worry about anything,
but in everything by prayer and supplication with
thanksgiving let your requests be made known to
God. And the peace of God, which surpasses all
understanding, will guard your hearts and your minds
in Christ Jesus.

Finally, beloved, whatever is true, whatever is
honourable, whatever is just, whatever is pure,
whatever is pleasing, whatever is commendable,
if there is any excellence and if there is anything
worthy of praise, think about these things ... and the
God of peace will be with you.

Philippians 4: 4–9

Jesus said.
"I will not leave you orphaned;
I am coming to you.
In a little while the world will no longer see me,
but you will see me; because I live, you also will live.
On that day you will know that I am in my Father,
and you in me, and I in you ..."
"Peace I leave with you; my peace I give to you.
I do not give to you as the world gives.
Do not let your hearts be troubled,
and do not let them be afraid."

John 14: 18–20, 27

Readings from other faith traditions and sources

You would know the secret of death.
But how shall you find it
unless you seek it in the heart of life?
The owl whose night-bound eyes are blind unto the
day
cannot unveil the mystery of light.

If you would indeed behold the spirit of death,
open your heart wide unto the body of life.
For life and death are one,
even as the river and the sea are one.

In the depth of your hopes and desires
lies your silent knowledge of the beyond;
And like the seeds dreaming beneath the snow
your heart dreams of spring.

For what is it to die but to stand naked in the wind
and to melt into the sun?
And what is it to cease breathing,
but to free the breath from its restless tides,
that it may rise and expand and seek God
unencumbered?

Only when you drink from the river of silence
shall you indeed sing.
And when you have reached the mountain top,
then you shall begin to climb.
And when the earth shall claim your limbs,
then shall you truly dance.

Kahlil Gibran (1883–1931)

Look to this day:
For it is life, the very life of life.
In its brief course
Lie all the verities and realities of your existence.
The bliss of growth,
The glory of action,
The splendour of achievement
Are but experiences of time.

For yesterday is but a dream
And tomorrow is only a vision;
And today well-lived, makes
Yesterday a dream of happiness
And every tomorrow a vision of hope.
Look well therefore to this day;
Such is the salutation to the ever-new dawn!

From Sanskrit (Hindu & Buddhist texts)

Yesterday is a memory,
tomorrow is a mystery and today is a gift,
which is why it is called the present.
What the caterpillar perceives is the end;
to the butterfly is just the beginning.
Everything that has a beginning has an ending.
Make your peace with that and all will be well.

Buddhist saying

As a man, casting worn-out garments,
taketh new ones, so the dweller in the body,
casting off worn-out bodies,
entereth into others that are new...
For certain is death for the born,
and certain is birth for the dead;
therefore over the inevitable
thou shouldst not grieve.

The Bhagavad Gita

On earth are signs for those whose Faith is certain:
And also in yourselves. Will you not then see?

And among His Signs is the creation of the heavens
and the earth and the diversity of your languages
and colours. Indeed, in that are Signs for those of
knowledge.

The Quran

My ego is like a fortress.
I have built its walls stone by stone
To hold out the invasion of God's love.
But I have stayed here long enough. There is light
Over the barriers. O my God—
The darkness of my house forgive
And overtake my soul.
I relax the barriers.
I abandon all that I think I am,
All that I hope to be,
All that I believe I possess.
I let go of the past,
I withdraw my grasping hand from the future,
And in the great silence of this moment,
I alertly rest my soul.
As the sea gull lays in the wind current,
So I lay myself into the spirit of God.
My dearest human relationships,
My most precious dreams,
I surrender to His care.
All that I have called my own
I give back. All my favourite things
Which I would withhold in my storehouse
From His fearful tyranny,
I let go.
I give myself Unto Thee, O my God. Amen

Howard Thurman (1899–1981)

It may be long, I will keep going
There may be danger, I will be brave
There may be storms, I will find shelter
There may be hunger, I will be given food
There may be rivers, I will cross them
There may be mountains, I will find a way through
There may be those to stop me, I will elude them
There may be great fear, I will ride with it
There may be loneliness, I will think of you
There will be a destination, I will reach it
I will have a home, I will return to it.

Author Unknown

Do not stand at my grave and weep
I am not there. I do not sleep.
I am a thousand winds that blow.
I am the diamond glints on snow.
I am the sunlight on ripened grain.
I am the gentle autumn rain.
When you awaken in the morning's hush
I am the swift uplifting rush
Of quiet birds in circled flight.
I am the soft stars that shine at night.
Do not stand at my grave and cry;
I am not there. I did not die.

Mary Elizabeth Frye (1905–2004)

We have dreamed dreams beyond our comprehending,
Visions too beautiful to be untrue;
We have seen mysteries that yield no clue,
and sought our goals on ways that have no ending ...
We have seen loveliness that shall not pass
We have beheld immortal destinies ...
Ay, we whose flesh shall perish as the grass
have flung the passion of the heart that dies
into the hope of everlasting life ...

But lo! Remains the miracle supreme,
That we, whom Death and Change have shown our fate,
We, the chance progeny of Earth and Time,
Should ask for more than Earth and Time create,
and, goalless and without strength to climb,
Should dare to climb where we were born to grope;

That we the lowly could conceive the great,
Dream in our dust of destines sublime,
And link of our moments to immortal hope ...
So, let us turn to the unfinished task
That earth demands, strive for one hour to keep
A watch with God, nor watching fall asleep,
Before the immortal destinies we ask.

Before we seek to share
A larger purpose, sublimer care,
Let us o'ercome the bondage of our fears,
And fit ourselves to bear
The burden of our few and sinful years,
Ere we would claim the right to comprehend
The meaning of life that has no end

Let us be faithful to our passing hours,
And read their beauty, and that light pursue
Which gives the dawn its rose, the noon its blue,
And tells its secret to the wayside flowers.

Sidney Royse Lysaght (1860–1941)

I've come to the end of life's busy road
I've put down the burden, I've cast off my load.
My spirit is free, my soul has wings
I'll pour from the throat of a bird that sings.
I'll ride on the wind, I'll float on the clouds
I'll twinkle with stars in night's velvet shroud.
I'll shine with the sun as it circles the earth
I'll be there at dawn when the new day gives birth.
I'll be with the snow fluttering down
Silently, softly, nature's crown.
I'll be in the rain as it falls on the earth
Cleansing, refreshing, priceless worth.
I'll ride on the ether, silent and free
A world of my own, please don't cry for me.

Maude Hurford (1888–1929)

Peace, my heart, let the time for parting be sweet.
Let it not be a death but a completeness.
Let love melt into memory and pain into songs.
Let the flight through the sky end in the folding of the
wings over the nest.
Let the last touch of your hands be gentle like the
flower of the night.
Stand still, O Beautiful End, for a moment, and say
your last words in silence.
I bow to You and hold up my lamp
to the light of Your way.

Rabindranath Tagore (1861–1941)

Life is a journey.
Death is a return to earth.
The universe is like an inn.
The passing years are like dust.

Regard this phantom world
As a star at dawn, a bubble in a stream,
A flash of lightning in a summer cloud,
A flickering lamp—a phantom—and a dream.

The Buddha, Vairacchedika 32

By the One in whose Hand is my soul, you will not
enter paradise until you believe, and you will not
believe until you love one another. Certainly, let me
inform you of that which may establish such things:
spread the greetings and peace among yourselves.

The Quran

O Allah, forgive our living and our dead, those who
are present among us and those who are absent, our
young and our old, our males and our females. Allah,
whoever You keep alive, keep them alive in Islam, and
whoever You cause to die, cause them to die with faith.
Allah, do not deprive us of the reward and do not
cause us to go astray after this.

O Allah, forgive us and have mercy on us, keep us safe
and sound and forgive us, honour our rest and ease
our entrance. Allah, admit us to Paradise and protect
us from the torment of the grave and the torment of
Hell-fire; make our grave spacious and fill it with light.
O Allah, if we are a doer of good, then increase our
good deeds, and if a wrongdoer, then overlook our bad
deeds. O Allah, forgive us and give us the steadiness
to say the right thing. Grant us security, glad tidings,
generosity and closeness to you.

Islamic funeral prayer

Prayers

Our Father in heaven,
hallowed be your name.
Your Kingdom come,
your will be done,
on earth as in heaven
Give us today our daily bread.
Forgive us our sins,
as we forgive those who sin against us.
Lead us not into temptation,
but deliver us from evil.
For the kingdom,
the power and the glory are yours.
Now and for ever. Amen.

The Lord's Prayer

Lord make me an instrument of Thy peace.
Where there is hatred, let me sow love;
Where there is injury, pardon;
Where there is doubt, faith;
Where there is despair, hope;
Where there is darkness, light;
Where there is sadness, joy.

O Divine Master, grant that
I may not so much seek to be consoled, as to console;
Not so much to be understood as to understand;
Not so much to be loved, as to love:
For it is in giving that we receive;
It is in pardoning, that we are pardoned;
It is in dying, that we awaken to eternal life.

Prayer of St Francis of Assisi (1226)

Oh, Great Spirit,
whose voice I hear in the winds
and whose breath gives life
to all the world, hear me.

I am small and weak.
I need your strength and wisdom.

Let me walk in beauty and make my eyes
ever behold the red and purple sunset.
Make my hands respect the things you have made
and my ears sharp to hear your voice.

Make me wise so that I may understand
the things you have taught my people.
Let me learn the lessons
you have hidden in every leaf and rock.

I seek strength, not to be superior to my brother,
but to fight my greatest enemy—myself.

Make me always ready to come to you
with clean hands and straight eyes,
so when life fades, as the fading sunset,
my spirit will come to you without shame.

Chief Yellow Lark, Lakota (1887)

Dear Lord, help me to live this day quietly, easily:
To lean upon your great strength trustfully, restfully:
To wait the unfolding of Your will patiently, serenely:
To meet others, peacefully, joyously:
To face tomorrow confidently, courageously.

Author Unknown

O God, take all our trials and sorrows
and use them to show us the nature of your joy;
Take all our sins, and, forgiving them,
use them to show us
the right ways and the pathways of true peace;
Take all our broken purposes and disappointed hopes
and use them to make your perfect rainbow arch;
Take all our clouds of sadness and calamity
and from them make your sunset glories;
Take our night and make it bright with stars;
Take our ill health and pain until they accomplish
as much as health could achieve;
Take us as we are with impulses, strivings,
longings so often frustrated and thwarted
and even with what is broken and imperfect
make your dreams come true,
through Him who made human life a sacrament,
of thorns a crown, of a cross a throne,
even through Jesus Christ our Lord, Amen

Rev Dr Leslie Weatherhead (1893–1976)

...That comes with parting, and the word, 'Goodbye.'
Dawn breaking after dreary hours of pain,
When I discovered that night's gloom must yield
And morning light breaks through to me again.
Because of these and other blessings poured
Unasked upon my wondering head,
Because I know that there is yet to come
An even richer and more glorious life,
And most of all, because Thine only Son
Once sacrificed life's loveliness for me.
I thank Thee, God, that I have lived.

Elizabeth Craven (1750–1828)

I thank Thee, God, that I have lived
In this great world and known its many joys;
The song of birds, the strong, sweet smell of hay
And cooling breezes in the secret dusk,
The flaming sunsets at the close of day,
Hills, and the lonely, heather-covered moors,
Music at night, and moonlight on the sea,
The beat of waves upon the rocky shore
And wild, white spray, flung high in ecstasy:
The faithful eyes of dogs, and treasured books,
The love of kin and fellowship of friends,
And all that makes life dear and beautiful.

I thank Thee, too, that there has come to me
A little sorrow and, sometimes, defeat,
A little heartache and the loneliness
God of life, there are days when the burdens we carry
chafe our shoulders and wear us down;
when the road seems dreary and endless,
the skies grey and threatening;
when our lives have no music in them
and our hearts are lonely,
and our souls have lost their courage.
Flood the path with light, we beseech you;
turn our eyes to where the skies are full of promise.
Amen.

Elizabeth Craven (1750–1828)

A prayer for loved one's we are leaving behind

Teach me O God, to trust you with life and death,
and though this is harder by far,
With the life and death of those that are dearer
to me than our own life.
Teach me stillness and confident peace
in your perfect will,
Deep calm of soul, and content in what you will do
with these lives.

Teach me to wait and be still,
To rest in yourself,
To hush all anxiety,
To lay in your arms all the wealth ... you have given me.

You love me and all souls that I love
With a love as far surpassing my own
As the glory of noon surpasses the gleam of a candle.
Therefore I will be still, and trust in You.

J S Hoyland (1750–1831) adapted

Hymns and songs

Nothing is lost on the breath of God
nothing is lost forever;
God's breath is love, and that love will remain,
holding the world forever.
No feather too light, no hair too fine,
no flower too brief in its glory,
no drop in the ocean, no dust in the air,
but is counted and told in God's story.

Nothing is lost to the eyes of God
nothing is lost forever;
God sees with love, and that love will remain,
holding the world forever.
No journey too far, no distance too great,
no valley of darkness too blinding,
no creature too humble, no child too small
for God to be seeking and finding.

Nothing is lost to the heart of God
nothing is lost forever;
God's heart is love, and that love will remain,
holding the world forever.
No impulse of love, no office of care,
no moment of life in its fullness,
no beginning too late, no ending too soon,
but is gathered and known in its goodness.

Colin Gibson

Guide me, O thou great Redeemer,
pilgrim though this barren land;
I am weak, but thou art mighty;
hold me with thy powerful hand;
Bread of heaven,
feed me now and evermore.

Open now the crystal fountain,
whence the healing stream doth flow;
let the fiery cloudy pillar
lead me all my journey through;
strong Deliverer,
be thou still my Strength and Shield.

When I tread the verge of Jordan,
bid my anxious fears subside;
bear me through the swelling current,
land me safe on Canaan's side;
songs of praises,
I will ever give to thee.

Bishop William Williams, (1800 – 1878)

He giveth more grace as our burdens grow greater,
He sendeth more strength as our labours increase,
To added afflictions He addeth His mercy,
To multiplied trials He multiplies peace.

When we have exhausted our store of endurance,
When our strength has failed ere the day is half-done,
When we reach the end of our hoarded resources
Our Father's full giving is only begun.

His love has no limits, His grace has no measure,
His power no boundary known unto men;
For out of His infinite riches in Jesus
He giveth and giveth and giveth again!

Annie Johnson Flint (1886–1932)

As the varied way of life we journey,
Come the plains and then the mountainside,
Come the days of joy when birds are singing,
And the world is fair and sweet and wide;
Then a deeper joy comes, overfilling,
From the everlasting throne of love,
And all other joy is but an echo
From the ever-blessed heights above.

There are shadows on the earthly pathway
Where, at times uncertainly, we tread;
In perplexity we halt and linger
Till our faith again is upward led.
For the heights of truth are ever calling,
And celestial radiance from afar
On our pilgrim way is gently falling
For our comfort where the shadows are.

In the days of peace and golden sunshine,
In the days of joy or days of woe,
There is confidence in him who holds us;
There is light to guide us here below.
And beyond await the heights of rapture
Where all earthly joys, transcended, fade
In the glory of the Saviour's presence,
In the home eternal he has made.

Lily Kells Sampson (1906–2000)

In heavenly love abiding,
no change my heart shall fear.
And safe in such confiding,
for nothing changes here.
The storm may roar without me,
my heart may low be laid,
But God is round about me,
and can I be dismayed?

Wherever He may guide me,
no want shall turn me back.
My Shepherd is beside me,
and nothing can I lack.
His wisdom ever waking,
His sight is never dim.
He knows the way He's taking,
and I will walk with Him.

Green pastures are before me,
which yet I have not seen.
Bright skies will soon be over me,
where darkest clouds have been.
My hope I cannot measure, my path to life is free.
My Saviour has my treasure, and He will walk with me.

Anna L Waring (1823–1910)

Soul of men! why will ye scatter
Like a crowd of frightened sheep?
Foolish hearts! why will ye wander
From a love so true and deep?

Was there ever kindest shepherd
Half so gentle, half so sweet,
As the Saviour who would have us
Come and gather round his feet.

There's a wideness in God's mercy
Like the wideness of the sea;
There's a kindness in his justice
Which is more than liberty.

There is welcome for the sinner,
And more graces for the good;
There is mercy with the Saviour;
There is healing in his blood.

But we make his love too narrow
By false limits of our own;
And we lose the tender shepherd
In the judge upon the throne.

For the love of God is broader
Than the measure of man's mind;
And the heart of the eternal
Is most wonderfully kind.

Frederick William Faber (1814–1863)

O love that wilt not let me go,
I rest my weary soul in thee;
I give thee back the life I owe,
that in thine ocean depths its flow
may richer, fuller be.

O light that followest all my way,
I yield my flickering torch to thee;
my heart restores its borrowed ray,
that in thy sunshine's blaze its day
may brighter, fairer be.

O joy that seekest me through pain,
I cannot close my heart to thee;
I trace the rainbow through the rain,
and feel the promise is not vain
that morn shall tearless be.

O cross that liftest up my head,
I dare not ask to fly from thee;
I lay in dust life's glory dead,
and from the ground there blossoms red
life that shall endless be.

George Matheson (1842–1906)

I know thee who thou art,
And what thy healing name;
For when my fainting heart
The burden nigh o'ercame,
I saw thy footprints on my road
Where lately passed the Son of God.

Thy name is joined with mine
By every human tie,
And my new name is thine,
A child of God am I;
And never more alone, since thou
Art on the road beside me now.

Beside thee as I walk,
I will delight in thee
In sweet communion talk
Of all thou art to me;
The beauty of thy face behold
And know thy mercies manifold.

Let nothing draw me back
Or turn my heart from thee,
But by the Calvary track
Bring me at last to see
The courts of God, that city fair,
And find my name is written there.

General Albert Orsborn (1886–1967)

Abide with me; fast falls the eventide;
The darkness deepens; Lord, with me abide;
When other helpers fail and comforts flee,
Help of the helpless, oh, abide with me.

Swift to its close ebbs out life's little day;
Earth's joys grow dim, its glories pass away;
Change and decay in all around I see
O Thou who changest not, abide with me.

I fear no foe, with Thee at hand to bless;
Ills have no weight, and tears no bitterness;
Where is deaths sting? Where, grave, thy victory?
I triumph still, if Thou abide with me.

Hold Thou Thy cross before my closing eyes
Shine through the gloom and point me to the skies
Heaven's morning breaks, and earth's vain shadows flee
In life, in death, O Lord, abide with me.

Henry Francis Lyte (1793–1847)

Be still, my soul: the Lord is on thy side.
Bear patiently the cross of grief or pain.
Leave to thy God to order and provide,
who through all changes faithful will remain.
Be still, my soul: thy best, thy heavenly Friend
through thorny ways leads to a joyful end.

Be still, my soul: the hour is hastening on
when we shall be forever with the Lord;
when disappointment, grief, and fear are gone,
sorrow forgot, love's purest joys restored.
Be still, my soul: when change and tears are past
all safe and blessed we shall meet at last.

Catharine Amalia Dorothea von Schlegel, (1697–1768)

Benedictions

Lord, be within me, to strengthen me,
outside to preserve me; over me, to shelter me;
beneath me, to support me; before me, to guide me;
behind me to steady me;
Round about me, to secure me.
Father, King of heaven and earth,
You are gentleness.
You are our protector,
You are our guardian and defender.
You are our courage.
You are our haven and our hope.
You are our faith, our great consolation.
You are our eternal life,
Great and wonderful Lord, God Almighty,
Merciful Saviour.

St. Francis of Assisi (1226)

May the road rise to meet you
May the wind be always at your back
May the sun shine warm upon your face
The rains fall soft upon your fields
And until we meet again, until we meet again
May God hold you in the palm of his hand
And until we meet again, until we meet again
May God hold you in the palm of his hand

May the sun make your days bright
May the stars illuminate your nights
May the flowers bloom along your path
Your house stand firm against the storm

And until we meet again, until we meet again
May God hold you in the palm of his hand
And until we meet again, until we meet again
May God hold you in the palm of his hand.

An Irish Blessing

We go in peace, journeying with God,
knowing that wherever we go,
wherever we are taken, whatever befalls us,
whenever we find ourself lost,
We simply turn, and know that God –
Creator, Friend, Companion –
stands with arms outstretched!

Author unknown

O Lord, support us all the day long,
until the shadows lengthen and the evening comes,
and the busy world lies hushed,
and the fever of life is over, and our work is done.
Then in your mercy grant us safe lodging,
a holy rest and peace at the last.

Cardinal Newman (1801–1890)

Go forth from this world:
in the love of God the Father who created you,
in the mercy of Jesus Christ who redeemed you,
in the power of the Holy Spirit who strengthens you.

May the heavenly host sustain you
and the company of heaven enfold you.
In communion with all the faithful,
may you dwell this day in peace. Amen.

From the Anglican Prayer Book

We go, trusting in a God who holds all creation,
nurturing each of our lives,
and who waits for us within the future.
May goodness and mercy
follow us all the days of our lives,
and may we dwell in God's house forever. Amen.

Author unknown

Whakataka te hau ki te uru
Whakataka te hau ki te tonga
Kia mākinakina ki uta
Kia mātaratara ki tai
E hī ake ana te atakura
He tio, he huka, he hau hū
Tīhei mauri ora!

Cease the winds from the west
Cease the winds from the south
Let the breeze blow over the land
Let the breeze blow over the ocean
Let the red-tipped dawn come with a sharpened air.
A touch of frost, a promise of a glorious day.

• • •

Kia tau ki a tātou katoa
Te atawhai o tō tātou Ariki, a Ihu Karaiti
Me te aroha o te Atua
Me te whiwhingatahitanga
Ki te wairua tapu
Ake, ake, ake
Amine

May the grace of the Lord Jesus Christ,
and the love of God,
and the fellowship of the Holy Spirit be with you all
Forever and ever
Amen.

Further reading

On Death & Dying: What the Dying Have to Teach Doctors, Nurses, Clergy & Their Own Families. Elisabeth Kübler-Ross. Scribner Book Company 2014.

The Long Goodbye. Megan O'Rourke. Riverhead Books 2012.

A Very Easy Death. Simone De Beauvoir. Pantheon Books 1985.

Praying Our Goodbyes: A Spiritual Companion Through Life's Losses and Sorrows. Joyce Rupp. Ave Maria Press 2009.

Good Grief: The Guide and Journal. Granger E Westberg; Jill Alexander Essbaum. Fortress Press 2019.

The Tibetan Book of Living and Dying. Sogyal Rinpoche. HarperOne (revised and updated) 2016.

A Grief Observed. C.S. Lewis. HarperOne 2015.

Last Words: Approaches to Death in New Zealand's Cultures and Faiths. Margot Schwass (Complier). Bridget Williams & the Funeral Directors Association 2005.

The Christian Art of Dying: Learning from Jesus. Allen Verhey. Eerdmans 2011.

Dying: A New Zealand Guide for the Journey. Sue Wood & Peter Fox. Calico Publishing 2006.

About the author

 Ian Kilgour is a Salvation Army officer and Christian minister with wide experience in pastoral care and the deeply human issues we all struggle with. Although now retired, he remains actively involved in church, chaplaincy, community and social justice work.

After a serious health event that caused him to face his own mortality, he gathered together the reflections that comprise this book—a work in which he was encouraged and assisted by the people of his home congregation, St. Heliers Presbyterian Church in Auckland.

Ian believes that everyone has the capacity to find meaning in life, to deepen their spirituality, and to become all they can be. He has an inclusive understanding of life in which everything and everyone is interconnected and of immense value.

Ian dedicates this publication to those whom he has had the privilege of laying to rest.

Endorsements

To those who reflectively read these pages as they knowingly approach the completion of their lives, and their death, Ian Kilgour has offered a map and a compass.

There is realism, compassion and inclusiveness in what he offers in this text—*The Art of Dying Well*. Not only that, he offers the wisdom and inspiration of others, as well as his own.

When we all harvest our experiences, offer thanks for all that has been and what we have learnt, then we can say a confident 'Yes' to whatever lies ahead, including death, where an embrace of undying Love awaits us.

Bishop Bruce Gilberd CNZM, S.Th., B.Sc.
Former Bishop of Auckland

Working in the pastoral care team environment of a retirement village, a need was identified for a resource that could offer people a pathway to help them face their fears about aging, illness and death.

Ian's writings allow people, to reflectively examine their lives and prepare for their final journey in a positive and hopeful way. His writings come from the heart and personal experience supported by inspirational writings, poetry and verse from throughout history and from all faith traditions and none.

The format Ian has chosen allows for those who may be struggling with concentration to absorb sections at their own pace and in whatever order they choose.

Patsy Cochrane, Chaplain,
St Andrew's Village

www.ingramcontent.com/pod-product-compliance
Lightning Source LLC
Chambersburg PA
CBHW031230120626
46545CB00003B/1065